La semplicità è la sofisticazione finale.
LEONARDO DA VINCI

Francisco LópezGuerra Almada

New York · Paris · London · Milan

Since I started to receive work commissions at a very young age,
I was always thrilled to accept them, but I am more grateful to feel your trust.
I receive it, and in return, I give you all my loyalty and friendship, forever.
Thank you, thank you.

Me enteré, con mucha satisfacción, pues Francisco López Guerra es amigo mío desde tiempos remotos, que este libro sería publicado y que tendría el privilegio de escribir unas palabras a manera de presentación.

La obra es, en parte, un relato de cincuenta años de arquitectura, de una persona estimable que se ha desarrollado, personal y profesionalmente, gracias a, y a pesar de, una vida que combina la tragedia de la muerte de sus padres a una edad temprana, con el acceso a vivencias y conocimientos en Europa, y la riqueza de sus raíces mexicanas.

La vida de Francisco es una mezcla de carácter y experiencia, misma que lo ha llevado a tener una enorme diversidad de pasiones e intereses, así como la valentía para perseguirlos con arrojo y pasión, recibiendo a su paso una larga serie de reconocimientos.

Y, con todo, este libro tiene otra parte, un mérito adicional que rebasa lo estrictamente académico y profesional: pues me parece que en su mira están los jóvenes, en particular los futuros arquitectos.

Para Pancho —como sus amigos le conocemos— las fuentes de motivación son indispensables para que surjan los verdaderos deseos, los talentos y las capacidades de diseñarse a uno mismo. Y es en la juventud cuando más impacto suelen tener.

Así fue para él.

Encontró en los recuerdos con su padre y en la relación con quienes con él trabajaron y convivieron, el ejemplo de construirse a sí mismo como persona, como maestro y como arquitecto.

El texto abre al lector su vida y a los jóvenes su experiencia. Estoy seguro de que las y los universitarios sabrán apreciar los contenidos de esta publicación, razón por la cual lleva el sello de esta casa de estudios.

Muchas felicidades, Francisco, por esta publicación.

Dr. Enrique Graue Wiechers
Rector
Universidad Nacional Autónoma de México

ACADEMIA NACIONAL DE ARQUITECTURA

FRANCISCO LOPEZ GUERRA ALMADA

Tuve el honor de conocer y tratar al gran arquitecto Francisco López Guerra padre, él me animó a conocer y querer la arquitectura, ahora Francisco López Guerra Almada es poseedor de una herencia, su ejemplo y ha desarrollado un lenguaje personal siendo el líder de un equipo de colaboradores profesionales de múltiples disciplinas.

Ha incursionado en la producción de espacios de diversos géneros y en los últimos años de manera particular en proyectos para museos y exposiciones tanto en nuestro país como en el extranjero; muchos de ellos logrados a través de concursos de arquitectura - que tanto falta hacen en México- como una forma de poner en juego de manera abierta las mejores ideas, entre los mejores arquitectos.

Dejar testimonio de la arquitectura de Francisco López Guerra Almada en una publicación de excelente calidad editorial nos da la oportunidad, y particularmente a las nuevas generaciones, de analizar y estudiar sus obras. Sobre todo, nos invita a conocerlas en persona para sentir y experimentar la composición espacial que es -en estricto sentido- una de las más importantes tareas del arquitecto. Como Presidente de la *Academia Nacional de Arquitectura* de la *Sociedad de Arquitectos Mexicanos*, en donde comparto con Francisco la categoría de *Académico Emérito*, celebro este libro por cumplir uno de los principales objetivos de la Academia: *conocer, reconocer y dar a conocer* la arquitectura como una disciplina de servicio para satisfacer las necesidades de espacios habitables.

JOSÉ F REYGADAS V. AE-SAM
Presidente

Ciudad de México, octubre 1, 2020
Día Nacional del Arquitecto

ARTISTIC DIRECTION + BOOK DESIGN
Loguer Design / Museotec

TEXT
Francisco LópezGuerra Almada

DESIGN STUDIO
Daniela Rocha

TRANSLATION
Annuska Angulo

PHOTO EDITOR
Isabel Hinojosa Quirós

PHOTO CREDITS
Loguer Design / Museotec
Juan Rodrigo Llaguno p. 31
Jorge Silva
Mariel Contreras Brizuela (Casa de la Cima)
Mattia Mognetti p. 156
Isabel Hinojosa p. 158
Mille Miglia l Official Photographer l Alessio Falzone Fotografo pp. 274–275

LOGUER ARCHIVE / UNAM
Francisco Treviño
Alfredo Hernández

pp. 10–11: La Libélula Project, Centro de Educación Ambiental, 2020

pp. 14–15: Winning project for the Mexican Pavilion at Expo Milan 2015

© 2021 Loguer Design
@loguerdesign www.loguer.com

© 2021 Mondadori Libri S.p.A.
Distributed in English throughout the World
by Rizzoli International Publications Inc.
300 Park Avenue South
New York, NY 10010, USA

ISBN: 978-88-918308-2-1
2022 2023 2024 2025 / 10 9 8 7 6 5 4 3 2 1

First edition: June 2021

This volume was printed at Editoriale Bortolazzi Stei S.r.l., Verona.
Printed in Italy

All rights reserved. No part of this publication may be reproduced, distributed, or transmitted in any form or by any means, including photocopying, recording, or other electronic or mechanical methods, without the prior written permission of the publisher.

---

p. 4

Francisco LópezGuerra Almada has been a friend of mine for a long, long time, so when I learned that this book would be published, and that I would have the privilege of writing a few words as a presentation, it gave me great satisfaction.

The book is partly an account of fifty years of architectural work of a well respected professional who has flourished thanks to, and despite of, the tragedy of his parents' death at an early age, the access to knowledge and experiences in Europe, and the richness of his Mexican roots.

Francisco's life is a mixture of character and experience which has led him to cultivate a wide range of passions and interests, as well as the boldness to pursue them with courage and resolution, receiving a long series of recognitions along the way.

And, however, this book has another side, an additional merit that goes well beyond the strictly academic and professional: it seems to me that it is very much directed to young people, particularly future architects.

For Pancho—as his friends know him—sources of inspiration are indispensable for bringing forth true desires, talents, and the capability to self-design. And it is in youth that inspiration has the deepest impact.

That is how it was for him.

In the memories of his father and in the relationship with those with whom he worked and lived, Francisco found the example of building himself as a person, as a teacher, and as an architect.

The text opens up his biography to the reader, and his experience to young people. I am sure that university students will appreciate the contents of this publication. That is why it bears the seal of this house of study.

Many congratulations, Francisco, for this book.

Enrique Graue Wiechers
President

National Autonomous University of Mexico

---

p. 5

FRANCISCO LÓPEZGUERRA ALMADA

I had the pleasure and the honor to know the great architect Francisco LópezGuerra senior. He was the one who inspired me to learn and love architecture. Now, Francisco LópezGuerra Almada is the heir to his legacy and example, developing his personal style as the head of a multidisciplinary team of professionals.

His practice extends to the creation of a wide range of spaces, particularly in the last few years, with projects for museums and World Expos, here and abroad, many of them won through competition—something we need so much in Mexico as a way to put the best ideas of the best architects into play.

Bearing testimony to Francisco's architecture in a book of excellent quality gives us, and particularly the new generations, the opportunity to analyze and study his works. Above all, he invites us to discover his work in real life, to feel and experience the spatial composition that is—in the strictest sense—one of the most important tasks of architects. As president of the National Academy of Architecture of the Society of Mexican Architects, where I share with Francisco the category of Emeritus Academic, I celebrate this book for fulfilling one of the main objectives of the Academy: to know, recognize, and publicize architecture as a discipline of service to meet the needs of living spaces.

José F Reygadas V. AE-SAM
President

Mexico City, October 1, 2020
National Day of the Architect

CONTENTS

Biography 14

Prologue 17
Jean-Claude Biver

I Wanted To Be An Architect 20
Francisco LópezGuerra Almada

ARCHITECTURE 33

Casa Glorieta
Casa Agapando
Casa Frontera
Casa Áncora
Casa Buganvilia
Casa Breña
Casa Cafetos
Casa del Árbol
Casa Cantera
Casa el Beso
Casa Sarunga
Casa Parque Vía
Casa del Arco
Casa el Secreto
Casa Gualdra
Casa las Terrazas
Rancho la Cosecha
Casa del Lago
Casa el Reflejo
Casa el Refugio
Casa la Orilla
Casa de la Roca
Rancho las Agujas
Casa Aguadoro
Casa de la Cima
Casa Pa'l Mar
PH Ixtapa
Club Porto Ixtapa

PAVILIONS & MUSEUMS 149

Latin American Pavilion Expo Zaragoza
Aguascalientes Pavilion
Mexican Pavilion Expo Milan
Explora, Science and Technology Center
Mexican Pavilion Expo Aichi
Veracruz State Science and Technology Museum
Interactive Museum Semilla
Desert Museum
Caracol Museum
Descubre

DESIGN 177

Fisher Island I
Fisher Island II
Fisher Island III
Vail Valley I
Vail Valley II
Creative Lab I
Creative Lab II
Brickell PH
Park Plaza
Chapultepec Golf Club
Yachts
Airplanes
Toluca International Airport Hangar
Il Architetto Hublot Watch

Competitions 245
Production Management 271
Loguer I Museotec Team 272
Epilogue 274

Continuous effort—not strength or intelligence—is the key to unlocking our potential.

WINSTON CHURCHILL

I dedicate this book to the loving memory of my beloved parents.

To Gina: without her love, none of this would have been possible.

To my children, for their pleasant company. Watching them grow up has been my greatest achievement.

To my grandchildren Georgie, Xavi, Jorge, Maxine, Paloma, Alejandro, and Fernanda. You are the joy in my life, and I leave you my advice: always go the extra mile.

BIOGRAPHY

Francisco LópezGuerra Almada won the "Luis Barragán" National Architecture Prize in 2000, presented by the Society of Mexican Architects, the College of Architects of Mexico, and the National Academy of Architecture, in recognition of his career and professional practice.

His studio is made up of an intergenerational and interdisciplinary team—architecture, engineering, museology, communication, and industrial, interior, graphic, and editorial designs—with representation in Mexico City and Miami.

The firm follows an architectural tradition of innovation in residential, corporate, public, cultural spaces, and comprehensive design solutions. One of their main strengths is to integrate form, function, and content according to the specific needs of each project. In informal learning projects, they carry out comprehensive planning, conceptualization, communication, design, production and assembly, evaluation, and monitoring. Loguer Design encompasses thirty-five years of accumulated experience, merging the services and skills of the companies Loguer SC (1976), Museotec (1989), and Desarrollos y Servicios de Ingeniería y Arquitectura (1998).

With more than fifty residential projects, ten museums, twelve public spaces, seven pavilions, offices, yachts, and publications, Loguer Design is an internationally recognized and award-winning firm. Winner of the competition to design the Mexican Pavilion at Expo Milan 2015, the firm received the Sustainability Award by the organizer of Expo Milan; the Award for the Best Pavilion of the Fifth World Water Forum 2009; the Gold Medal for the Latin American Pavilion at Expo Zaragoza 2008; the Gold Medal for Content and Silver Medal for Design at the Mexican Pavilion at Expo Aichi 2005; and winner of the Open Competition for the Development of the Executive Project of the New Public Library of the State of Jalisco (2005).

Among the most outstanding achievements of his studio are the Science and Technology Museum of Xalapa (1992), Explora in León (1994), Descubre in Aguascalientes (1996), Semilla in Chihuahua (2004), the Desert Museum in Saltillo (1997), and the Aquarium of Veracruz (2002).

Il "totomoxtle

LA FORZA DELL'IDEA
e la buccia di mais e la pelle del padiglione

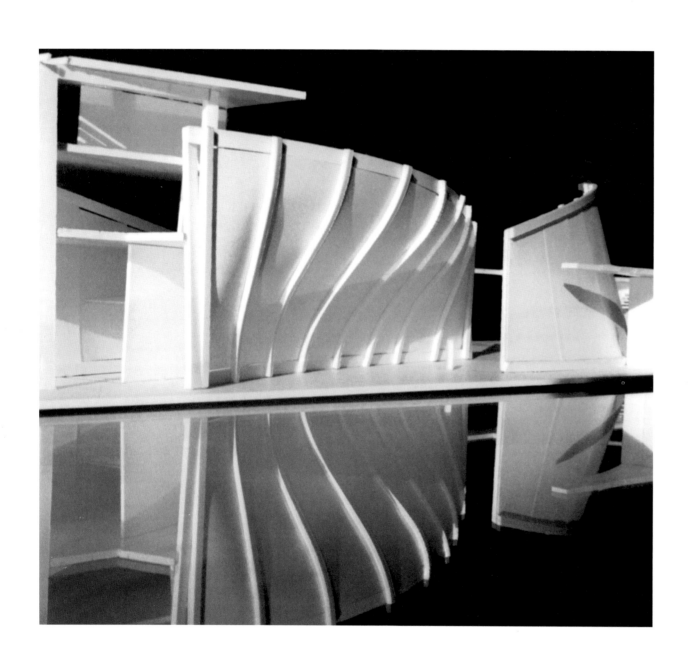

Jean-Claude Biver
HUBLOT

PROLOGUE

I have observed the world of design and its variants throughout my lifetime. I have understood the balance with which it is possible to transmit satisfaction and wellbeing to the customer after finding equilibrium between tradition and innovation. This search requires constant effort of struggle and observation. Learning without stopping, and on that way of knowledge, to lose and not tire.

I have lived a similar journey and I understand Pancho's path. Since the day we met, I have observed his passion for design and for the functional parts, I was a witness of how he designed two watch collections that have been successful. We agree that simplicity is not emptiness, you must find order and balance in the complex, seeking to achieve clarity and efficiency, as well as depth and everlasting beauty. His architectural vision based on finding the strength of an idea will always be a theme for the younger generation to reflect upon. We also know that there is no future without innovation.

Pancho learned the trade of architecture by accompanying his father, in the same way one learns to become a carpenter, a winemaker or a cheesemaker, it's a family tradition. His is an incredible mix of the academic, his cultural roots, together with great teachers, and the European influence where his Italian passion stands out.

With this book, I gladly join him in celebrating his 50 years as an architect. His youth along with his experience, manifested in his prolific work keep him in good spirits and with that joy of learning that distinguishes him. I know his father died very young, but from here, in Geneve, I can tell you that he is very happy.

I WANTED TO BE AN ARCHITECT

FRANCISCO LÓPEZGUERRA ALMADA

LÓPEZGUERRA SENIOR'S FIRST BUILDING IN MEXICO CITY, FROM 1949, IS RECOGNIZED AS ONE OF THE MOST SIGNIFICANT HISTORIC CONTRIBUTIONS TO MEXICAN ARCHITECTURE

**Success is not final, failure is not fatal:
it is the courage to continue that counts.**

Winston Churchill

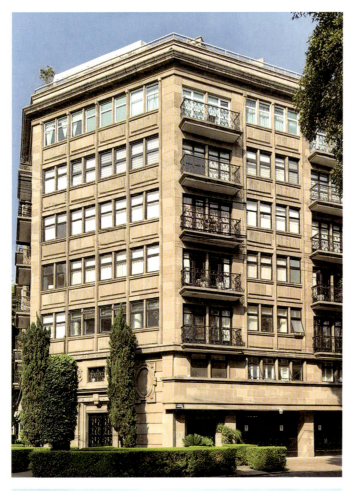

I have nothing to offer except my love for life and my work. At age seventy-one, I can look back and retrace the steps of my path. This story emerges from the footsteps of others: those of my family and my teachers.

I was born in 1949. As my mother, in her womb, prepared me for life, my father finished his first building, located on the corner of Insurgentes Avenue and Londres Street, which today marks, along with other buildings, the beginning of modern Mexican architecture. In 1950, when I took my first steps and finally experienced verticality in my own body, the LOGUER building—named after the contraction of my father's last names, López and Guerra—was already fully functional, and became, symbolically, my other backbone.

During my childhood, every Saturday I would walk with my father to his workplace. It was fascinating to me, to walk into his office in the building with which I share my birth year, and look at pencils, drafting tables, rulers, and rolls of paper. I followed him on his visits through the construction sites, and while playing with stones, mortar, and sand, I met the masons, the electricians, the carpenters, the plumbers. Sharing these moments, I discovered the craft of architecture, my vocation, and the significance of work.

Over time, I have understood the importance and permanence of my father's work. In particular, there are two examples that stand out: the family house in León, Guanajuato, designed and built in 1953 in the style of an Italian villa with Palladian proportions, which, despite the different use—today it is a newspaper's headquarters—continues to highlight the strength of its architecture; and an apartment building in Polanco, built in 1963, elevating its form and geometry in the purest European *pan coupé* tradition, and still preserving elegance in its maturity.

From my father, I also inherited my interest in cars. He was Enrique "el Rudo" Ortiz Peredo's partner, and he used to invite the Italian drivers of the Carrera Panamericana for lunch. All this was fascinating for my young mind. At the age of twelve, he took me to two car races: the 12 Hours of Sebring and the 24 Hours of Le Mans. On these occasions he made me feel like his friend and partner-in-crime; we shared rooms and schedules, something unusual in our everyday life.

My father was generous by sharing his world: in his profession, his interests, and friendships, the family was always included and welcomed. Life gave me a short time with him: he died when I was fifteen. But it was enough to build the pillars that made me into the person I am today. I recall the painful memory of removing his belongings and closing his office. My mother made me realize that I had to learn how to work and take charge of the maintenance and accounting of the buildings. When I finished high school, I had no doubt: I wanted to study architecture.

Maybe because I lost my father so early, when I went to university I had a huge need for support and a pat on the back. Life's wonderful compensation was to allow me to find teachers who became great mentors. I knocked on the door of the already well-known architect Pedro Ramírez Vázquez, who offered me a job as a library assistant in his office. Don Pedro received architectural publications from all over the world; as he spoke only Spanish, he marked the articles he was interested in and I sent them to be translated; then, with his consent, I would take a photocopy for myself. Nourished with so much information, I broadened my vision of architecture, which helped me refine my sensitivity, observe new technologies, and advance my training. Just listening to him, being in his company, was of enormous value. I admired that his entire work was based on pre-Hispanic and colonial culture and heritage. He had remarkable knowledge of this country's tradition and sought to honor it in his work. I was fortunate to accompany him on some of his travels around the world and learned from him something so fundamental that to this day I never get tired of repeating it: architecture is lived through the body; the power of the space has to be felt.

Don Pedro Ramírez Vázquez was president of the Organizing Committee of the XIX Olympiad, and I was very close to him when there was a surge of great architectural work built in Mexico for the 1968 Olympics. In coordination with José Ramírez O'Erlich, one of my jobs was to bring international visitors to see the new buildings. At that time, the Camino Real hotel had just been built in Polanco, causing a great worldwide stir as one of the most important buildings of that time. I approached the architect Ricardo Legorreta to understand his vision of color and space. From then on, a beautiful and very long friendship was born between the two of us. The extraordinary thing about these builders is that each in his own way embraced the powerful and rich elements of our Mexican culture to build contemporary architecture, something Ricardo explained with immense joy, and Don Pedro, with sobriety and conviction.

At the age of twenty-one, three fundamental events occurred. The first was that I met Gina. Everything that has happened in my life since then has to do with her. She is my life companion and she has defined who I am today.

The second was that I built my first building. I was able to achieve this because I had an exceptional role model for overcoming challenges and love for work, but also because of the limitless support of the architects and builders who had collaborated with my father. They were always there for me, having my back and sharing their knowledge. Sheltered by my friends' trust and the resources of the partners who gave me courage and self-confidence, I started my career as a house builder and rolled into the endless work cycle of architecture: a constant starting and finishing, fueling up on life every time a new opportunity appeared, and dying a little at the end of each project.

The third was that, when I was twenty-one, my mother died. She was a woman of common sense, joy, and extraordinary power, who always knew how to guide us, especially after she was widowed. One of her favorite things that she would repeat

ARCHITECT RICARDO LEGORRETA VILCHIS

"The group of Mexican architects that developed their work between the thirties and sixties participated in the configuration of a vigorous and creative culture. They formed a generation characterized by solid preparation and strong commitment to architecture, and to society. Francisco LópezGuerra, Pancho's father, was highly esteemed for his work and brilliant career, cut short by his premature death.

His son has recovered and developed this legacy, creating modern and valuable architecture. Without losing sight of his personal talent, he has incorporated the contributions of his collaborators, who together conform his professional studio. His works are a great contribution to Mexico's contemporary architecture.

Francisco LópezGuerra has created open spaces and plazas in large-scale and of great complexity. However, he has also produced more intimate, smaller scale works. His work enriches its surroundings; instead of being turned inward, they tend to become popular urban centers. His works integrate contemporary and traditional, urban and nature, and local with international.

I was very pleased to compete against him in several national and international projects and to participate in this summary of his work, that deserves wide recognition and appreciation."

Ricardo Legorreta Vilchis

ARCHITECTS PEDRO RAMÍREZ VÁZQUEZ AND FRANCISCO LÓPEZGUERRA ALMADA

to me, again and again, was: "Pancho: anyone can start a project; some know how to continue, but very few can finish." My sister and I became our only family; she never let me feel alone, she had a beautiful sense of humor and was a constant presence in my life, pleasant and constructive. Now, as I write these lines I pay a tribute to her; just a few days ago she left this world, but she will live in my memory with gratitude forever.

When I stopped working with Ramírez Vázquez, Fernando Pérez Salazar, my father's friend, took me to meet the architect Juan Sordo Madaleno, who remembered his friendship with my father at school and put me in the hands of José Adolfo Wiechers, better known as Pepón. At that time, the Plaza Satélite shopping center was being built, and I was an assistant to the building's resident engineer. This allowed me to develop a very deep relationship with Pepón, as a friend and teacher. His technical knowledge was vast, his geometry impeccable, as were his formulas to solve any problem; he was a complete professional with a great human quality.

Soon after, I became independent and set up my own studio. I took the drafting tables and instruments that I had kept from my father's office. I kept the name of his studio in his honor and made a new design based on what I learned from Don Pedro: the logo resembles a pre-Hispanic fretwork representing the cycle of life, with a line that starts and ends constantly.

I was fortunate to collaborate with José Emilio Amores in 1994, when we did the remodeling of the Alfa Cultural Center, in the city of Monterrey. He was a formidable cultural mover and shaker in our country, founding professor of the Monterrey TEC University, and far ahead of his time. He knew about the importance of non-formal education and interactive museums. Working with him was extremely important because it broadened my vision on education as a social responsibility, and I made use of his modern and avant-garde teachings when I extended my practice to public spaces.

I have nothing but genuine admiration for the architect Augusto H. Álvarez and his great work. It is no coincidence that one of the most emblematic and safest buildings in Mexico City, the Torre Latinoamericana, was his work. But what I remember the most with great affection is an anecdote regarding the intimate. Augusto was born in Merida, he came to study in the capital, and when he entered the school, my father was on his way out. One day he told me that when he arrived in town he had very few resources and that my father gave him the first suit he ever wore in his life.

These are my foundations, my roots, and the lineage to which I belong. I am grateful for being fortunate enough to have met all the people who enabled me to develop as I did, and now I am proud to present my work as the sum of everything that I owe to them.

THE HOUSES

It is said that space is defined by light. But it is the air that inhabits the space and collects the sound of the surrounding nature. This explains why my first proposal for a house always begins around the terrace and the garden, especially with a privileged climate like ours, which allows us to stay outdoors most of the year, and contained spaces with controlled temperatures are not used that often. To make the most of architecture, there has to be plenty of air, light, and outdoor space where we are free to draft the project proposal to our liking.

I was a swimmer as a child and my close relationship with water allows me to perceive it as an element that leads to enjoyment and physical activity. In this sense, especially in weekend houses, water can be integrated into pools and fountains that enhance the space with joy and freshness.

To get to know our clients better, we invite them for lunch at my house and talk about their needs and dreams. A house is the fruit of a long-standing desire, full of emotions and expectations.

I continue and renew the tradition I come from by building with stones, just as our ancestors did, and by using an earthy color palette. I transform the concept of pre-Columbian patio and colonial patio into terraces. I search for local materials that react to the changes in temperature and humidity of the site. The ashlars made of tepetate—naturally compressed volcanic clay—work as insulators. The stone must be light-colored to increase the light's intensity. The wood gives the warmth that the environment needs. In addition to design, the other challenge is the use of technologies as key resources to control natural and artificial light.

Thanks to the success of our homes, we accepted invitations to collaborate with clients of various nationalities and to work abroad. This is where we faced new challenges: we had to adapt to extreme climates and previous constructions. This prompted us to create multifunctional spaces that perform differently depending on the season.

The selection of houses presented here is primarily for family living. Therefore, the most important spaces are those where the transition between the interior and the exterior takes place since the greatest use happens around the table and collective activities. It fills me with satisfaction to know that we have created places full of beauty and functionality so that the family unit is strengthened.

INTERIORISM (SKETCH)

SKETCH FOR COMPETITION

INTRODUCING THE CASA MEXICANA PROJECT TO
THE MEXICAN AND FRENCH PRESIDENTS

INTRODUCING THE MEXICAN PAVILION FOR EXPO MILAN WITH AMBASSADOR RICARDO AMPUDIA AND
THE ITALIAN PRIME MINISTER MATTEO RENZI TO THE MEXICAN PRESIDENT ENRIQUE PEÑA NIETO

INTERIOR ART

One of the challenges in design has been to transform intimate and functional spaces to give them the importance they did not have before. Until the 1950s, all sinks were ceramic, with a limited choice of models. The most daring ones only varied in color. This changed in a very interesting way: the sink, integrating the use of new materials, became the perfect opportunity for talented artisans to develop unique pieces. A common-use object that stays in the client's private space becomes a beautiful piece, an artistic complement in bathrooms.

Stairs, which must above all be spacious and functional, are a channel for innovation. We transformed them into sculptural spaces where they become great sources of natural light that allow us to trace contemporary lines, posing new challenges at the structural level. Thanks to developments in geometry and structural calculation, we can propose sophisticated designs beyond conventional structures to our clients, and this has led us to self-supporting designs, or even to reverse the logic of stairs, and hang them from an upper structure.

THE IMPORTANCE OF COMPETING

Competing is a verb that must be used constantly. It is a muscle that must be exercised as much as possible, and as early as possible: it increases your creativity, opens your mind, strengthens the spirit. It is a constructive activity in many ways.

The first time I entered an international competition, I was very young. I worked very hard on it and when I got the results, I was sorely disappointed. Ramírez Vázquez called me and told me something that proved to be true time and time again: "The more you lose, the closer you get to winning." Another fundamental life lesson learned.

We are constantly trying to participate in competitions and open calls. The competitors are big international names in architecture who force you to look for new design possibilities, and that is very challenging. Sometimes you get lucky and opportunities open up to win, as has happened in Spain, the United States, and Italy, among other countries. But the essential thing about competing is learning how to lose, examining why you lost, analyzing the successful projects, understanding the logic of their concepts, which at the end of the day is very rewarding.

The public library of Guadalajara University was a significant experience for us. We worked very hard on the proposal as a literal and metaphorical door to knowledge and to the cultural complex of the Guadalajara University, where it is located. The building's function was to house the collection and to allow the circulation of a large number of users. We put a lot of work on the way natural, zenithal, diffused light was used. The solution of using the overhead light that bathed the entire interior space was undoubtedly the driving force that gave us the chance to win the international competition and build the project. However, at the last moment, the owner of the property decided to change the facade without our consent. So even if you are a worthy victor, there are battles that you can't win.

CULTURE AS A VOCATION

Some experiences mark a "before" and "after" in life: the visit to the Museum of Science in Boston is one of them. Gina and I understood the importance of interactive museums as a cornerstone of informal learning. This gave us a chance to work together, which enriched us as a couple, and as an architectural firm, it made us think of museums and cultural centers as propitious places to awaken vocations.

We started with the Xalapa Science and Technology Museum in 1992, the first interactive museum in Mexico. It had such a significant social and educational effect that it opened the door for the development of new spaces where I could explore another type of architecture without losing the notions of light, sound, and air which I have been working with all my life. Seeing families, and especially children, moved by the visit to the museum increased my sense of social responsibility in architecture.

Museums are spaces that serve society; they encourage discovery and understanding, an experience that will stay with you forever. It is a great motivation as a human being, but especially as a Mexican. I was pleased to present our proposals to several Mexican presidents and prime ministers of other countries.

The strength of our idea is simple: the container should serve the content. It seems like a simple statement, but it is a controversial point because there

PEDRO RAMÍREZ VÁZQUEZ, FRANCISCO LÓPEZGUERRA ALMADA, RAFAEL TOVAR Y DE TERESA, AND RICARDO LEGORRETA VILCHIS

FRANCISCO LÓPEZGUERRA ALMADA WITH MADAME ANNE HIDALGO

FRANCISCO LÓPEZGUERRA ALMADA, RAFAEL TOVAR Y DE TERESA, AND HIS WIFE MARIANA GARCÍA-BÁRCENA

"When I saw the Mexican Pavilion at Expo Milan '15, I saw the evolution of Mexican architecture. I could see a bridge between the twentieth and twenty-first centuries.

Pancho assimilated the roots of the eloquent cultural power of Mexico, and achieved a synthesis of contemporary architecture on historical bases. The always sharp Italian critics in their observation have qualified it as 'La Forza dell'Idea.'

The influence of Pedro Ramírez Vázquez and Ricardo Legorreta is reflected in an eloquent contemporary manifestation where modern design evolves without leaving behind the roots of our origins, of our history."

Rafael Tovar y de Teresa

is a vision of architecture that seeks the opposite: to create emblematic and representative buildings with budgets that often exceed the content they house. We have learned that the strength of content is the true mission of the museum, and that is more transcendent than the architectural vanity of going down in history. Rather than doing showy buildings with enormous technical challenges, we seek to create an architectural experience in the service of society, one that meets the needs of the people who visit them. That's where Gina's work is fundamental. Her company, Museotec, creates the museographic script after extensive research. From this, we obtain clear ideas to produce powerful concepts that we use to compete for commissions. But this means more to me than a professional achievement. Gina gave me a home to make the family we have: three children and seven grandchildren; when I design the museums or pavilions for which she produces the script, I feel that now it is me who offers her a home for her ideas to inhabit. We have learned to build a family and a life's work together; we have learned to overcome obstacles and become stronger.

To this day we have participated in fifteen contests to build museums, and we have developed eight with that same spirit. Highlighted among them: Explora in León, Guanajuato (1994), Descubre in Aguascalientes (1996), Semilla in Chihuahua (2004), the Desert Museum in Saltillo, Coahuila (1997), and the Aquarium of Veracruz (2002). We have also taken part in several international fairs, among which I highlight three: the Expo in Aichi, Japan, in 2005, the Expo in Zaragoza, Spain, in 2008, and the Expo 2015 in Milan, Italy. When we think of presenting Mexico to the world, we focus on the national heritage our country has to offer.

Japan's theme was "Nature's Wisdom"—the Japanese ideogram's meaning could also be understood as the "The Love to Earth Exhibition." Mexico is the fourth leading country in biodiversity in the world, and we searched for a concept that would strengthen and convey the exhibition content of the pavilion. The facade of the building was a screen that, as the afternoon light entered, projected images of our wildlife: jaguars, cactus, and butterflies, among many other beauties. This provided movement and dynamism to the facade of the building and credited us with recognition.

In Zaragoza, Spain, the subject was "Water and Sustainable Development." We won the competition to build the Latin American pavilion. We developed the concept around the idea of temperate forests and rainforests, and titled it "In the Rain." Our idea was to reproduce the geometric trace from the sap of a leaf that resembles an aerial view of rivers.

The Milan Pavilion in 2015 was also very relevant. The theme was "Feeding the Planet, Energy for Life." We suggested that Mexico should showcase maize, one of its great contributions to the world. The facade is inspired by the totomoxtle (the corn husk). Our proposal was a textile membrane that allowed a play of transparency in the daytime, and a source of light at night. It was one of the most visited pavilions, and it won the Gold Medal at the Universal Design Exhibition. This allowed me to talk with the Italian prime minister, who was so enthusiastic about the work that he rounded out my presentation for the president of Mexico when we walked through the pavilion. I was also invited to the School of Architecture of the Polytechnic University of Milan to talk about my work philosophy.

Due to this social architecture work, in the year 2000, the president of Mexico, Ernesto Zedillo, awarded me the "Luis Barragán" National Architecture Prize in recognition of my professional career. I was very moved to receive this honor since the jurors of the prize are all colleagues from the Society of Mexican Architects, the College of Architects of Mexico, and the National Academy of Architecture.

OPERATING MACHINES

The museums were our starting point to get us closer to other types of buildings. As our team became stronger, we began to look for new areas of development for architectural projects: those that have their own logic and dynamism. We had built offices to enhance creativity and improve the quality of life, optimizing and embellishing areas where people spend fourteen hours a day. What we learned about space as an element of social function in museums helped us to consider buildings as what I call "operating machines." We create a spatial and architectural feeling by always keeping in mind our core philosophy: the container has to serve the purpose of the content. Each space is like a gear that should work with the flow of people and activities to create the best environment possible. For each purpose, we look for advice with specialists to better understand specific needs. In this sense, some projects have been developed in collaboration with Antonio Toca, whose architectural vision is always timely in context, history, and advice. His assessment was fundamental in the library of the Guadalajara University in Jalisco, the Pavilion of Mexico in Aichi, the Latin American Pavilion in Zaragoza, the Church of Our Lady of Guadalupe in Indiana, the monument to Martin Luther King in Washington, DC, the Casa Ajaracas in the Historical Center, and the Hospital General of Mexico City.

Before becoming a proposal, each specific project, with its defined particularities, is an opportunity to learn something new. The offices, the Hospital General of Mexico City, the Chapultepec Golf Club, the Club Porto Ixtapa, and the Hangar of Toluca International Airport are examples of this.

TIME FOR DREAMS AND NEW PROJECTS

I have always had a great interest in the mechanism and design of watches, not so much as jewelry but as design pieces. The detail of the cases and the combination of materials offer fantastic possibilities. On one occasion, when visiting the Hublot workshop, I was lucky enough to meet the CEO, Mr. Biver. I told him about my work, about my interest in the pieces, and we agreed that I would design a watch. In my design, I played with the materials and the face, with a ceramic case and a leather strap. When the pieces were sold out and I wanted more to be produced, Mr. Biver explained to me that the value of the limited edition is that no more pieces are ever produced. That led me to the design of another version, now with titanium and a fabric strap. Perhaps it was in that symbolic act of creating an object to measure time that I entered another time in my life: that of fulfilling dreams and fostering new ones.

Since I was a child, I have had a very close relationship with Italy. My father invited Italian car drivers for lunch at our Cuernavaca house. Furthermore, he had a friend, Commendatore Orlando Crotti, with whom he had a very intense epistolary relationship. His letters were a topic of conversation and celebration in our house. Fifteen years ago we decided to look for the famous Commendatore, and I found an octogenarian gentleman of great human quality. He gave me a fatherly hug and welcomed me with the same tenderness as if I was his own son. It was very moving. He revealed to me things that I didn't know about my father: how they began their friendship after my father commissioned five Alfa Romeo cars, which started the brand's presence in Mexico. Also, they built houses together on Lake Maggiore. Moreover, my sister lived for a year in Italy, and when she returned—I was still a child—I was fascinated by everything she told me: the language, the songs, her experience, plus all the pictures she brought with her. All this left a great impression on my soul.

The passion for automobiles that I inherited from my father made me think, for a while, that I wanted to be a driver. I always felt tempted to be part of that world. But my mother sold my dad's cars and she said to me: "Let them go, someday you'll have yours." The truth is that my reality required something different. On the way, I met Gina, and with her, I envisioned the possibility of forming a family, which was a much more significant enterprise. So the dream of cars had to wait until it was time to fulfill it.

Thanks to my cousins, Fernando and Alejandro Gayou Almada, who are more like brothers than cousins—we named our third child in honor of the former—I was able to recover one of the cars that belonged to my father; it was not good for much, but the sentimental value was priceless because the original invoice was in my father's name. I fixed it, and I started dreaming of racing it at the Mille

Miglia Storica. The Mille Miglia was born in 1927 and then suspended for security reasons in 1957. Its beauty was that the race was held on real roads, rather than on a circuit. In the late 1970s, this initiative was revived under the name of Mille Miglia Storica, which today is the most prestigious classic car race in the world. Only cars that competed in some edition of the first period, between 1927 and 1957, can take part in it. I soon knew that I would never be able to take my father's car to the race because it simply didn't comply with the regulations, but a friend introduced me to a person who owned a car that did, and this opened up the possibility of fulfilling my dream.

When I was sixty-eight, I had a health scare. It was a complicated period in my life that I could not have crossed without Gina's unconditional love and without my children's affection: Francisco, a man of strong convictions who holds a unique relationship of respect and love with nature; without the sagacity of Gina, who knows how to open paths and for whom nothing is impossible; without the son I gained in Javier, my son-in-law; without Fernando, a Mexican like few, who fights for his country and his ideals; without Ale, who has brought her family's strengths to ours and made us the recipients of her patience and prudence; without the joy of my grandchildren Georgie, Xavi, Maxine, Jorge, Paloma, Alejandro, and Fernanda; and without the good wishes, messages, and prayers of my friends. It happened as everything does, with the good and the not so good, and at sixty-nine, after so much work and effort, life gave me the chance to fulfill the dream of Mille Miglia Storica. My wish was no longer only mine: Gina joined me, and my friend Tinaco Artigas with his wife, children, and grandchildren, and it was quite an adventure, which was repeated a year later, in the Dolomites, with Gina, my daughter, my son-in-law, and my grandchildren. Those were days of sheer happiness. There, everything came together: the love for life that my parents gave me, my childhood, my love for Italy, my friends, and my family.

Now I'm starting another adventure. It's like I've been pruned: I feel more vigor and energy to live to my fullest. It is time for new shoots, to work and heal. I know now it is the time for miracles and plenitude. I understand better than ever why I like to work and learn, and why from a very young age *I wanted to be an architect.*

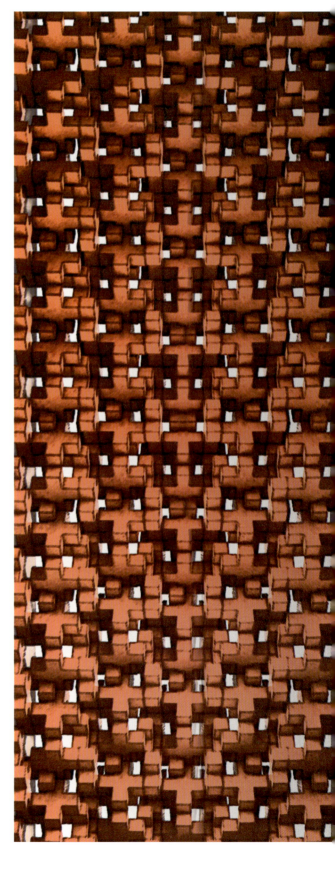

The basic design principles of the game *la matatena*—a Pre-Hispanic name that means "to fill with stones" in Náhuatl—and the correlation between its parts motivated me and have been a source of creativity. Today I observe with great interest its similarity in the relationship between spaces and components with the design solutions adopted in the proposals for the lunar stations and later on planet Mars.
This subject has always been on my mind.

ARCHITECTURE

CASA GLORIETA
MEXICO CITY, MEXICO

CASA AGAPANDO
MEXICO CITY, MEXICO

CASA FRONTERA

MEXICO CITY, MEXICO

CASA ÁNCORA

MEXICO CITY, MEXICO

CASA BUGANVILIA
MEXICO CITY, MEXICO

CASA BREÑA

MEXICO CITY, MEXICO

CASA CAFETOS

MEXICO CITY, MEXICO

CASA DEL ÁRBOL

MEXICO CITY, MEXICO

CASA CANTERA
MEXICO CITY, MEXICO

CASA EL BESO

MEXICO CITY, MEXICO

CASA SARUNGA

MEXICO CITY, MEXICO

CASA PARQUE VÍA

MEXICO CITY, MEXICO

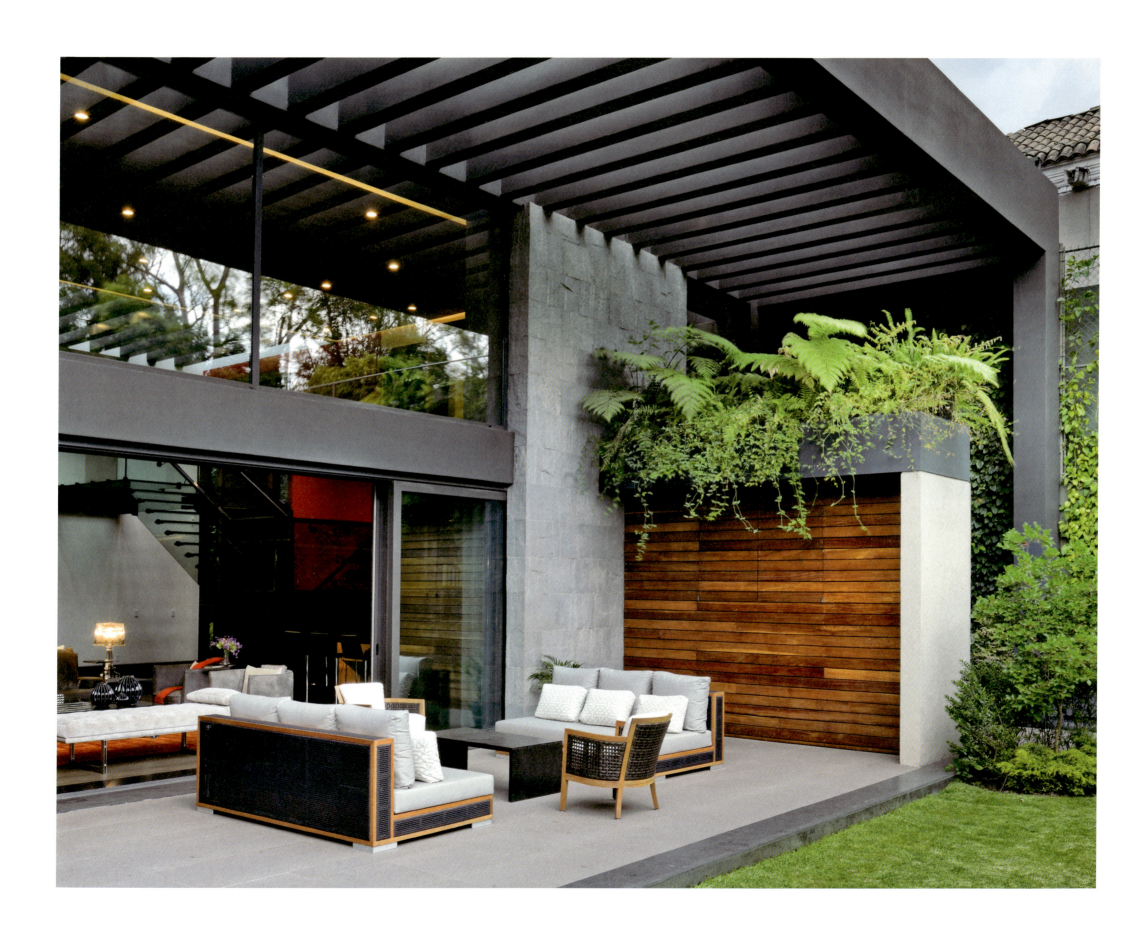

CASA DEL ARCO

MALINALCO, STATE OF MEXICO, MEXICO

CASA DEL ARCO   MALINALCO, STATE OF MEXICO, MEXICO

CASA EL SECRETO

MALINALCO, STATE OF MEXICO, MEXICO

CASA GUALDRA
MALINALCO, STATE OF MEXICO, MEXICO

RANCHO LA COSECHA

ACATITLÁN, STATE OF MEXICO, MEXICO

CASA DEL LAGO
VALLE DE BRAVO, STATE OF MEXICO, MEXICO

CASA EL REFLEJO

VALLE DE BRAVO, STATE OF MEXICO, MEXICO

CASA LA ORILLA

VALLE DE BRAVO, STATE OF MEXICO, MEXICO

CASA DE LA ROCA

VALLE DE BRAVO, STATE OF MEXICO, MEXICO

RANCHO LAS AGUJAS

VALLE DE BRAVO, STATE OF MEXICO, MEXICO

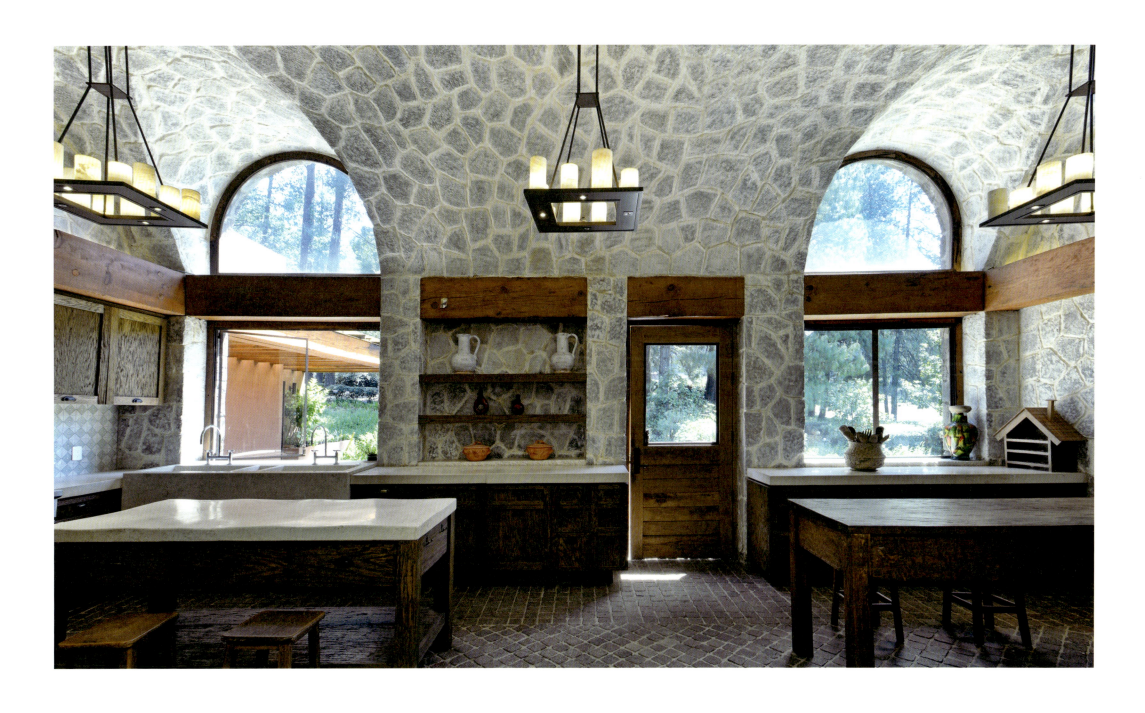

CASA DE LA CIMA
LEÓN, GUANAJUATO, MEXICO

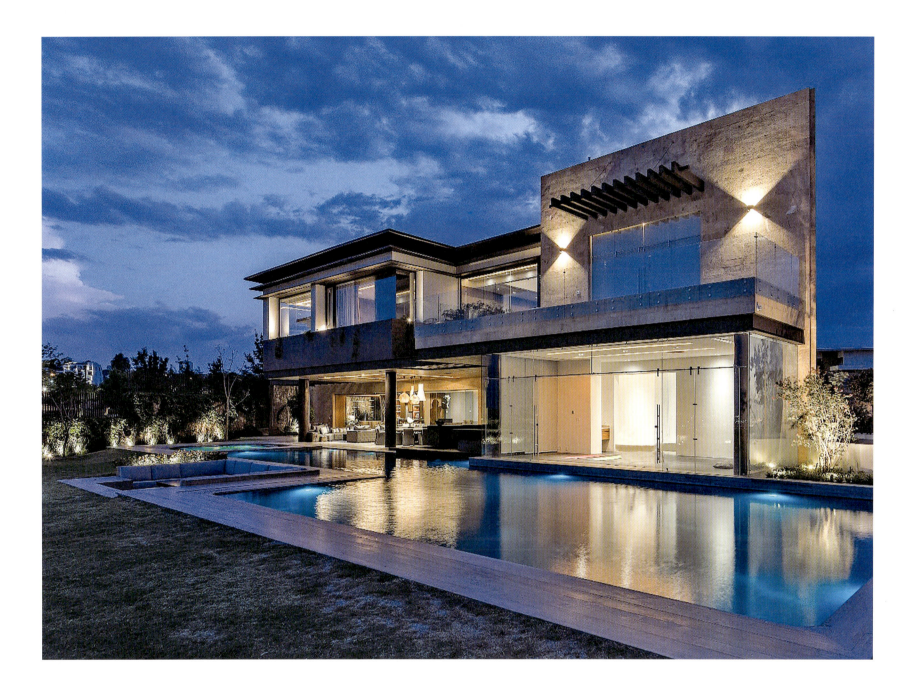

CASA PA'L MAR

IXTAPA ZIHUATANEJO, GUERRERO, MEXICO

PH IXTAPA

IXTAPA ZIHUATANEJO, GUERRERO, MEXICO

CLUB PORTO IXTAPA

IXTAPA ZIHUATANEJO, GUERRERO, MEXICO

PAVILIONS & MUSEUMS

When architecture and content
come together in a single message,
the strength of the great communicator is achieved.

CONCEPTUALIZATION AND MUSEOGRAPHIC DESIGN DEVELOPED BY GINA AND THE MUSEOTEC TEAM

Georgina Larrea, Francisco's wife, as a liberal arts student, pursued a bachelor's degree in art history and museology.

"Everything that happened after I turned twenty-one," says Francisco, "was in collaboration with Gina. Many friends joke about it and tell me that I got extremely lucky with her. Our dreams are the light that illuminates everything, and we always had the courage to share concepts, not only to enjoy our relationship but to develop ideas as a team."

In 1989, when Gina and Francisco took their eldest son, Francisco, to study English at a Boston school, they had a life-changing experience.

"On that occasion," Francisco recalls, "we visited the Science Museum in Boston, an extraordinary interactive museum. It was an eye-opening experience that made us realize the potential of informal learning in Mexico, and we decided to make it our goal to reproduce that exercise for the youth and children of our own country. In the process, I learned how to subject the architecture of a museum to the needs of its content. We succeeded in finding a good option at an adequate cost."

The first building of this kind became a reality in the Museum of Science and Technology in the state of Veracruz, in the city of Xalapa.

"Today I am convinced that Gina's knowledge of art history and museology, and her enormous capacity as a researcher, were the fundamental bases that allowed us to find solutions for a lot of those proposals that went from drawings on paper to becoming real buildings; without this sound foundation, we would not have been able to generate the solid ideas that allowed us to compete successfully. The story of this shared experience, seen today in retrospect, well admits the metaphor that Gina gave me reins, saddle, and horse, to go out riding . . . together."

The concepts developed by LópezGuerra conform a whole architectural and museological vision of its own, which became very relevant in present-day Mexico.

"Vanity," explains Francisco, "sometimes gets the best of architects, who want to make history with a very significant building. Gina, with all her reasoning, made me understand that architecture must be relegated by force to the contents inside the museum. This helped us a lot because it allowed us to build financially sound projects, such as the one in Jalapa. Striving to balance our relationship as a couple, we overcame adverse situations, and that was very lucky for us. Today I see many young couples who under any pretext throw it all out the window because they have not built defense mechanisms against obstacles; you need to hold on a little bit to overcome them and find your balance. It sounds easy, this metaphor for success: 'It is a pleasure to learn to build together.'"

LATIN AMERICAN PAVILION

EXPO ZARAGOZA 2008 | ZARAGOZA, SPAIN

GOLD MEDAL FOR CONCEPT DEVELOPMENT & INNOVATION

FRANCISCO LÓPEZGUERRA ALMADA WITH VICENTE LOSCERTALES, GENERAL SECRETARY OF BIE, IN THE AWARD CEREMONY FOR THE GOLD MEDAL FOR CONCEPT DEVELOPMENT & INNOVATION FOR THE LATIN AMERICAN PAVILION

AGUASCALIENTES PAVILION
LANDSCAPE AND POETRY | AGUASCALIENTES, MEXICO

Mexico City, October 26, 2017

ProMéxico was born as an institution to promote Mexico abroad. Promote it, first and foremost, as a country favorable to foreign investment; promote the export of its best products and services; promote leading Mexican companies in our own country that can compete successfully with the best and strongest in the world.

To undertake this important task, ProMéxico chooses its best allies and benefits from their contributions and commitment to Mexico. This is how this institution's fruitful and long-lasting relationship with Francisco LópezGuerra Almada was born. A talented Mexican architect, his love for Mexico honors us.

LópezGuerra understood, a long time ago, Mexico's essence which ProMéxico exports: contemporary, dynamic, and global. In all the architectural projects he has led for us, he has clearly captured this reality without losing sight of our cultural heritage and ethnic diversity. In this task, he joins his teachers and friends Pedro Ramírez Vázquez and Ricardo Legorreta.

But something distinguishes Francisco: his enormous ability to convey with his work the process of Mexican architecture's evolution. His works are, without a doubt, a bridge between the twentieth and the twenty-first centuries.

Expo Aichi in Japan, Expo Zaragoza, and Expo Milan share the hallmarks of their author: a modern design that reflects the ancient cultural heritage of Mexico. This fortunate balance is one of the reasons why our pavilions are among the most striking and popular at international exhibitions.

For me, as ProMéxico General Director, and as a Mexican citizen, it is a pleasure and an undeserved privilege to participate in the presentation of this book that brings together the work of a talented professional, of an architect committed to his country, whose work reflects the best values of his generation.

Paulo Carreño King
General Director

Ciudad de México, 26 de octubre de 2017

ProMéxico nació como la institución encargada de promover a México en el exterior. Promoverlo, en primera instancia, como un destino propicio para la inversión extranjera; promover la exportación de sus mejores productos y servicios; promover a las empresas mexicanas líderes en nuestro país y que pueden competir, de tú a tú, con las más fuertes y prestigiosas del mundo.

Para acometer esta importante tarea, ProMéxico elige a sus mejores aliados y se beneficia de sus aportaciones y compromiso con México. Así nace la relación fructífera y duradera de esta institución con Francisco López-Guerra, talentoso arquitecto mexicano, que nos distingue con su amor por México y lo mexicano.

El arquitecto López-Guerra entendió, desde hace muchos años, la esencia del México contemporáneo, dinámico y global que ProMéxico exporta. En todos los proyectos arquitectónicos que ha liderado para nosotros, ha plasmado con claridad esta realidad sin perder de vista nuestra herencia cultural y riqueza étnica. Se suma en esta tarea a sus maestros y amigos, Pedro Ramírez Vázquez y Ricardo Legorreta.

Pero algo distingue a Francisco: su enorme capacidad de transmitir con su trabajo un proceso de evolución de la arquitectura mexicana. Sus obras son, sin duda, un puente entre el siglo XX y el siglo XXI.

Expo Aichi en Japón, Expo Zaragoza y Expo Milán comparten sellos distintivos propios de su autor: un diseño moderno al tiempo que reflejan la ancestral riqueza cultural de México. Este afortunado equilibrio da cuenta de que nuestros pabellones se encuentren entre los más vistosos y los que más audiencia atraen en las exposiciones internacionales.

Para mí, como director general de ProMéxico y como mexicano, es un gusto y un inmerecido privilegio participar en la presentación de este libro, una obra que reúne el trabajo de un profesionista talentoso; de un arquitecto comprometido con su país, cuyo trabajo refleja los mejores valores de esta generación.

Paulo Carreño King
Director General

**Success is walking from failure to failure
with no loss of enthusiasm.**

Winston Churchill

MEXICAN PAVILION

EXPO MILAN 2015 | MILAN, ITALY

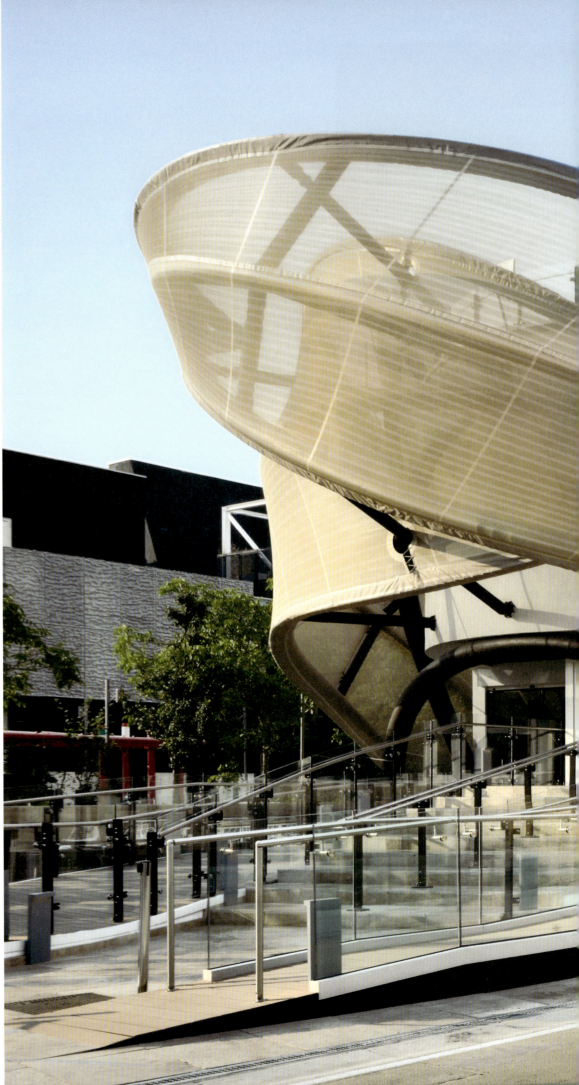

It is the possibility of having a dream come true that makes life interesting.

Paulo Coelho

EXPLORA, SCIENCE AND TECHNOLOGY CENTER

LEÓN, GUANAJUATO, MEXICO

WITH THE GOVERNOR OF THE STATE OF GUANAJUATO CARLOS MEDINA,
THE PRESIDENT OF THE BOARD OF TRUSTEES JORGE CARLOS OBREGÓN,
RAFAEL YAMÍN, AND HÉCTOR RODRÍGUEZ APARICIO

MEXICAN PAVILION
EXPO AICHI 2005 | AICHI, JAPAN

VERACRUZ STATE SCIENCE AND TECHNOLOGY MUSEUM

XALAPA, VERACRUZ, MEXICO

OPENING CEREMONY WITH THE GOVERNOR DANTE DELGADO AND THE PRESIDENT CARLOS SALINAS DE GORTARI

INTERACTIVE MUSEUM SEMILLA

CHIHUAHUA, CHIHUAHUA, MEXICO

DESERT MUSEUM

SALTILLO, COAHUILA, MEXICO

CARACOL MUSEUM

ENSENADA, BAJA CALIFORNIA, MEXICO

DESCUBRE

AGUASCALIENTES, AGUASCALIENTES, MEXICO

WITH THE GOVERNOR OF AGUASCALIENTES LICENCIADO OTTO GRANADOS AND THE GOVERNMENT SECRETARY CARLOS RUVALCABA

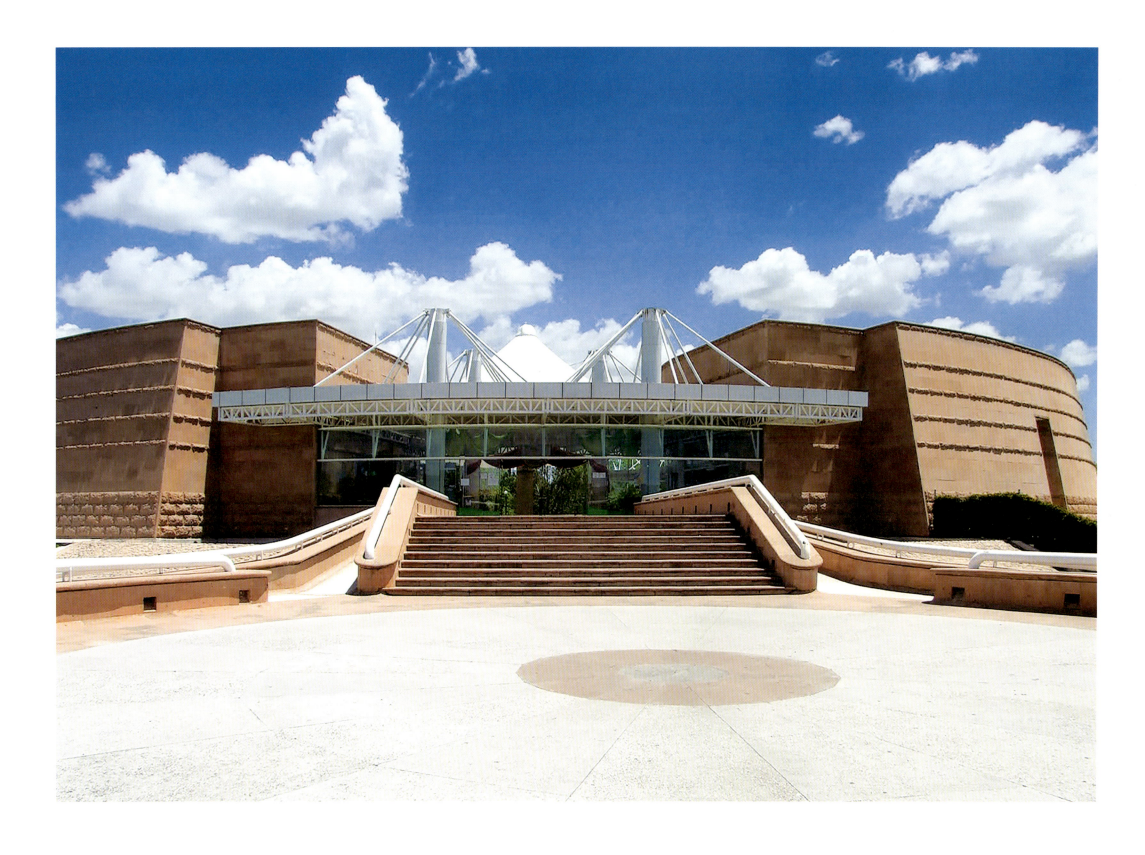

DESIGN

FISHER ISLAND I
MIAMI, FLORIDA, USA

FISHER ISLAND II
MIAMI, FLORIDA, USA

FISHER ISLAND III
MIAMI, FLORIDA, USA

VAIL VALLEY I
VAIL, COLORADO, USA

VAIL VALLEY II
VAIL, COLORADO, USA

CREATIVE LAB I
MEXICO CITY, MEXICO

CREATIVE LAB II
MEXICO CITY, MEXICO

INTERIOR DESIGN
OFFICES & RECREATIONAL SPACES

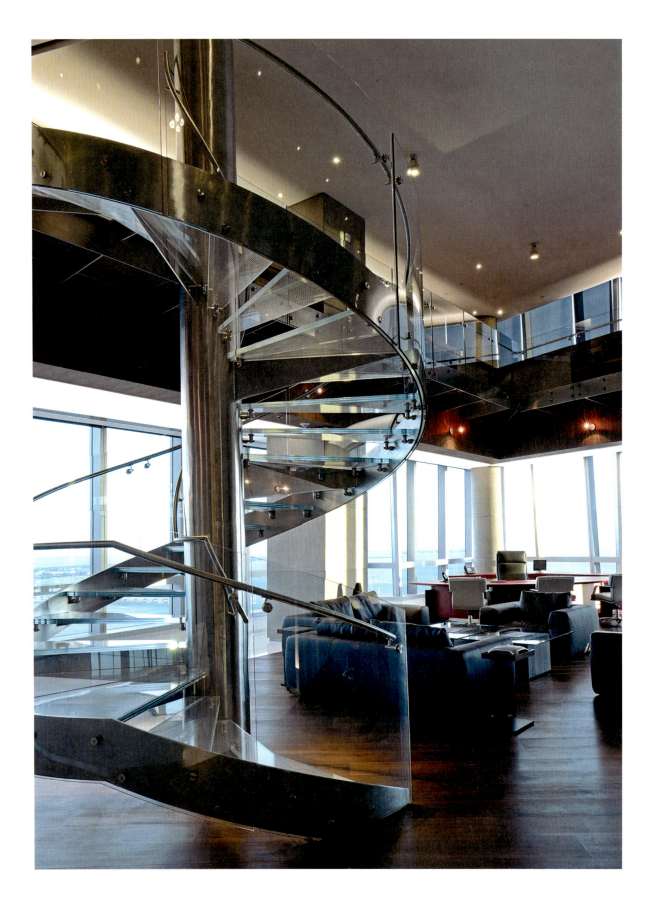

BRICKELL PH
MIAMI, FLORIDA, USA

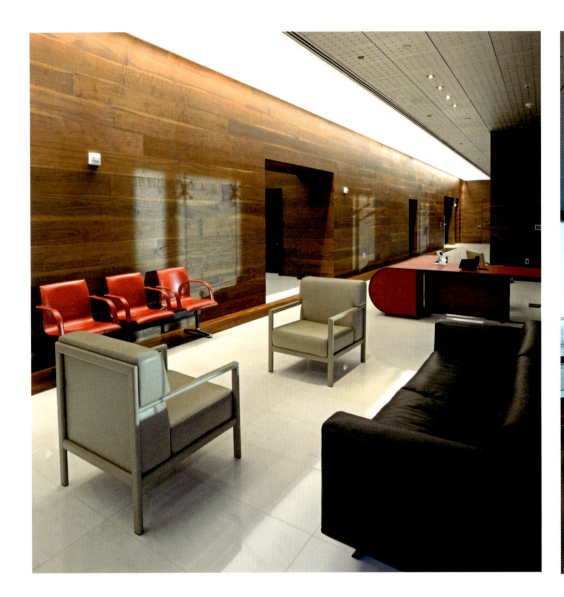

PARK PLAZA
MEXICO CITY, MEXICO

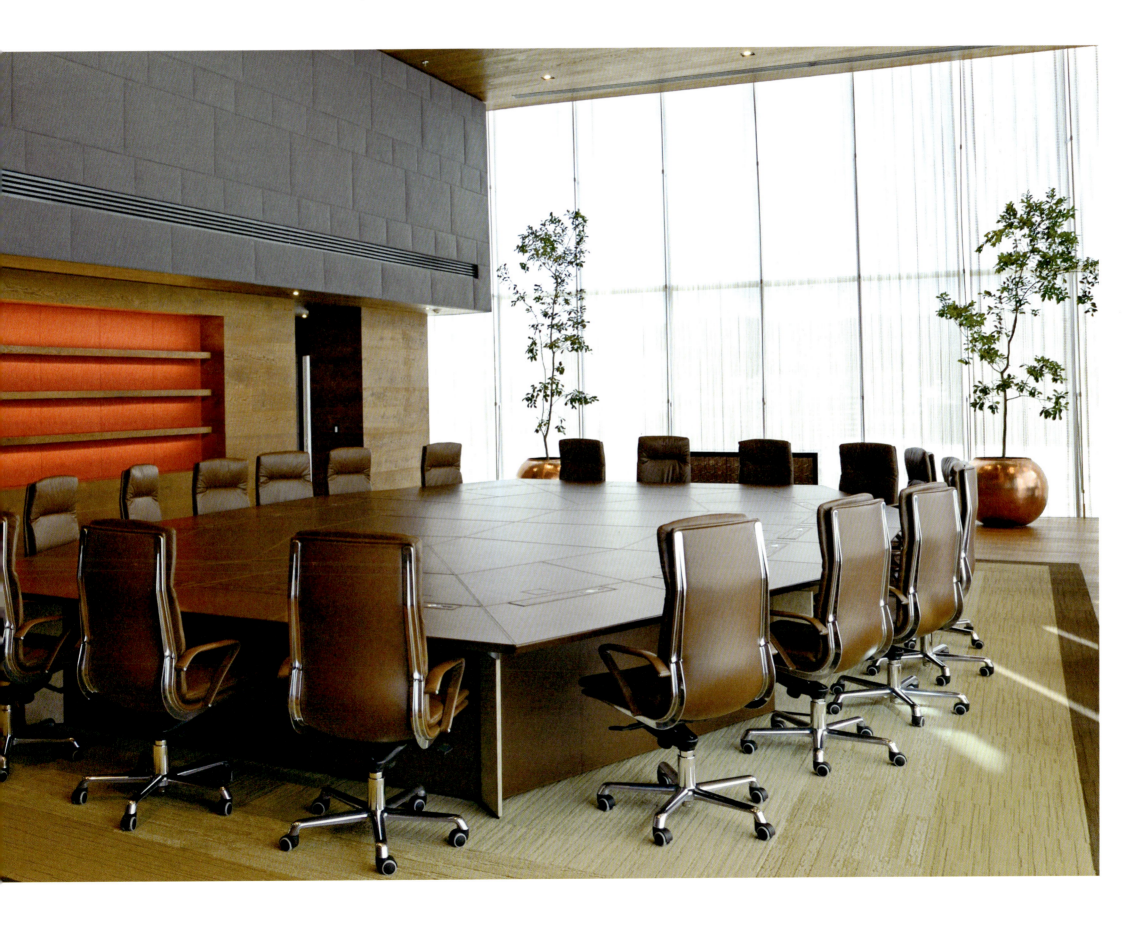

CHAPULTEPEC GOLF CLUB

MEXICO CITY, MEXICO

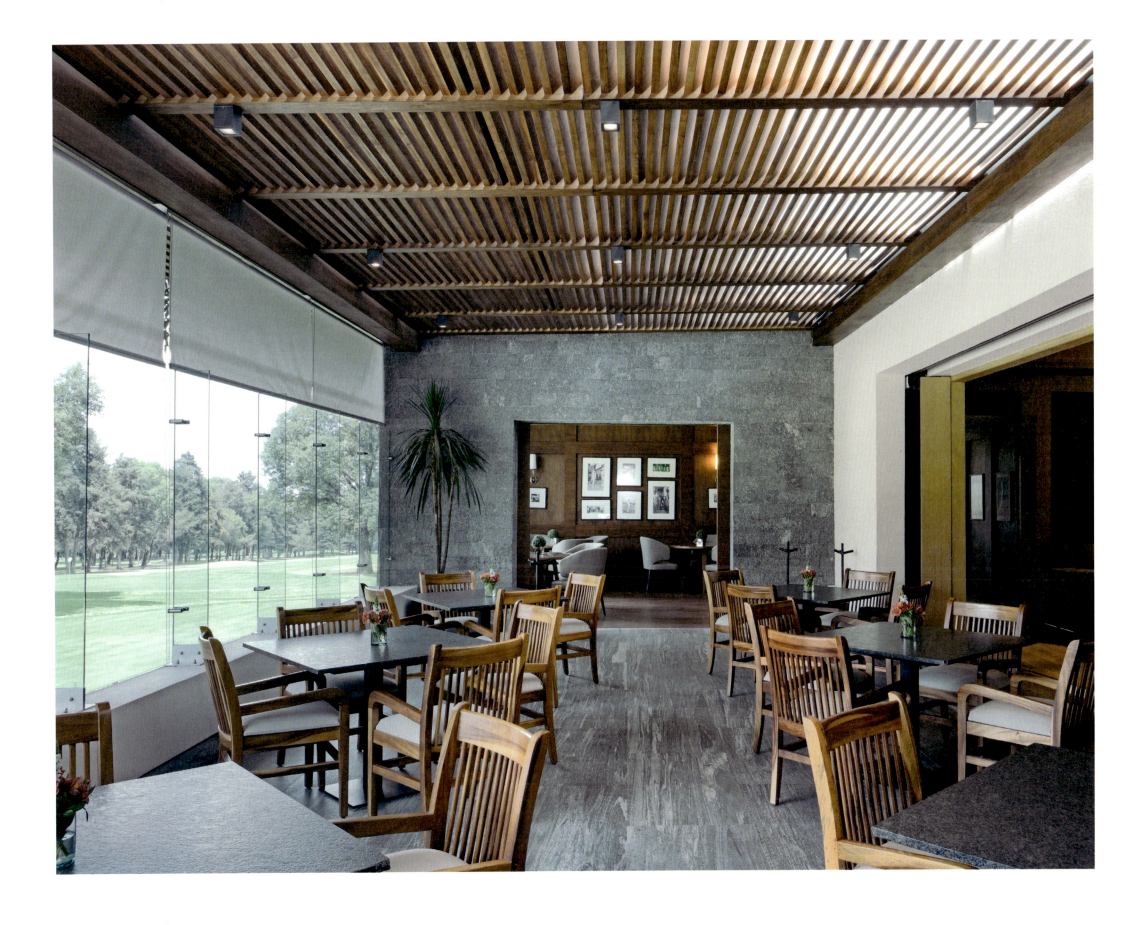

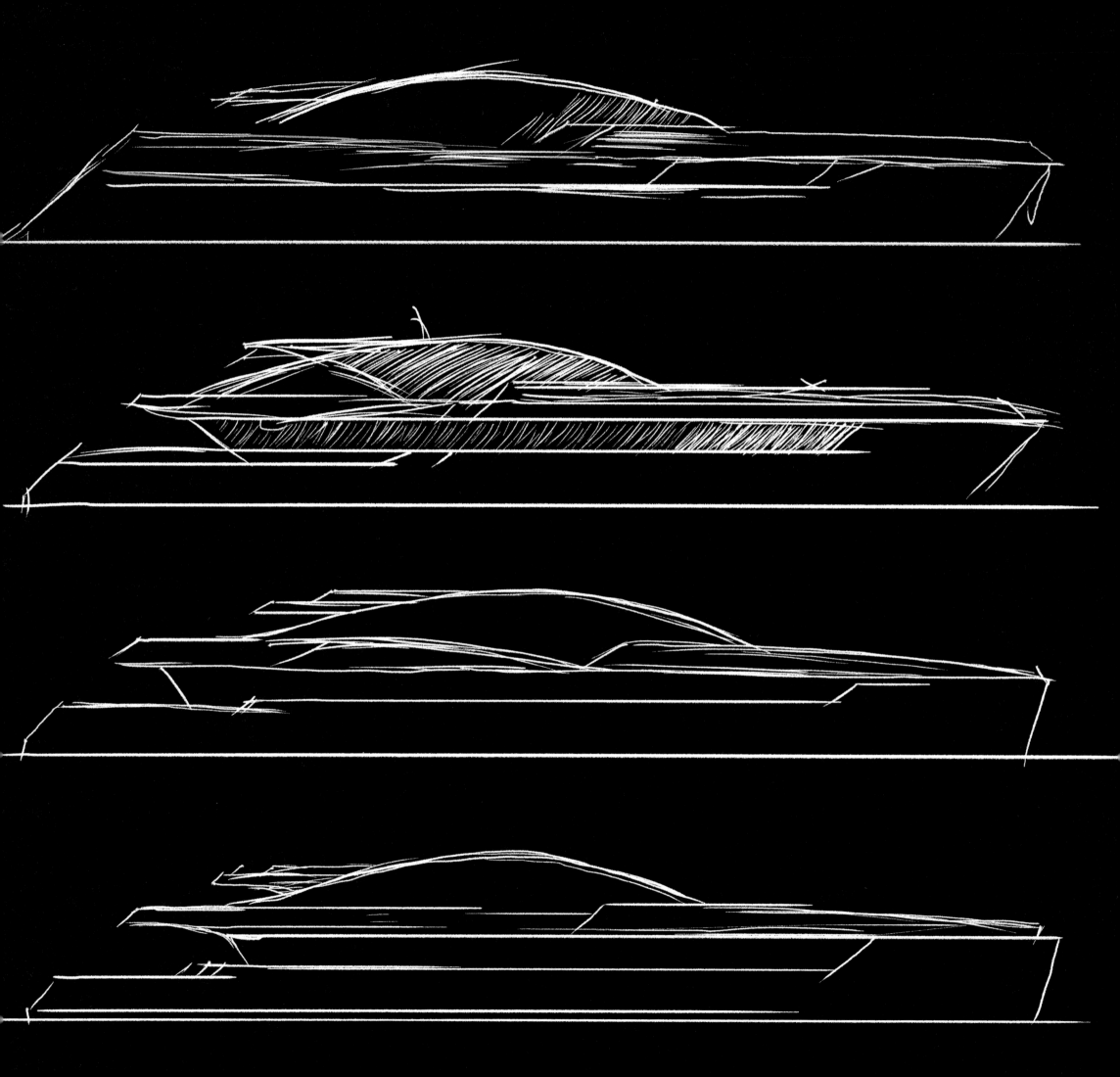

YACHTS & AIRPLANES
INTERIOR DESIGN

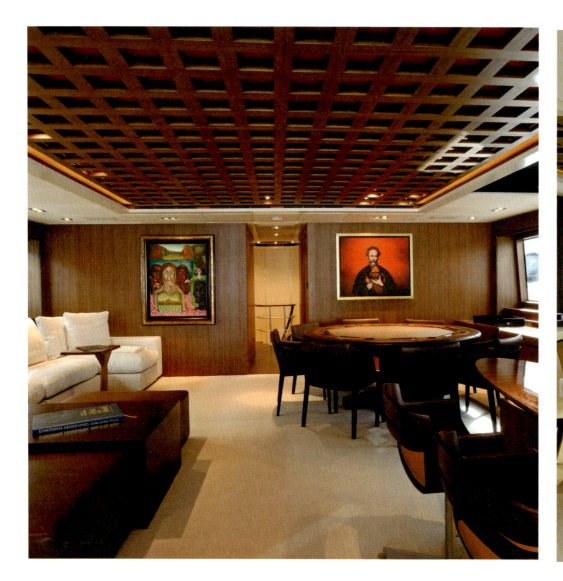

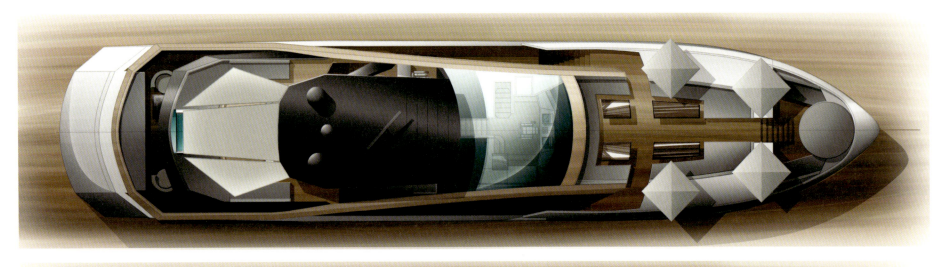
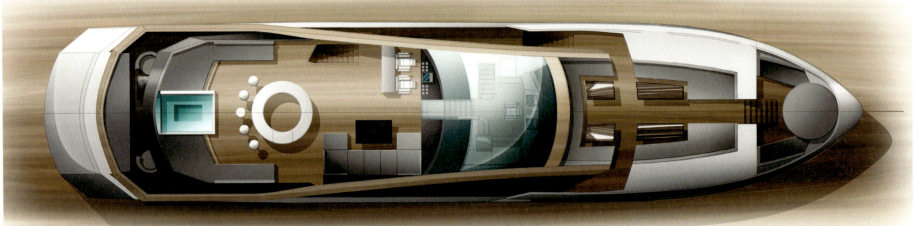

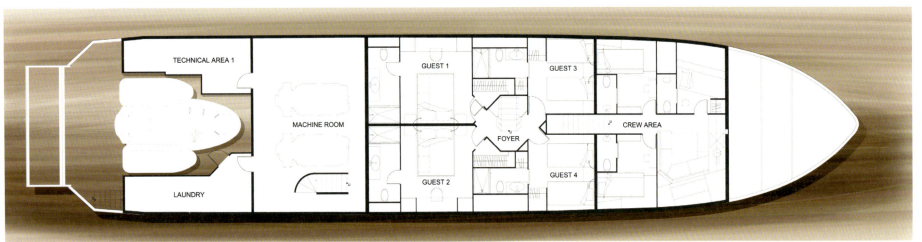

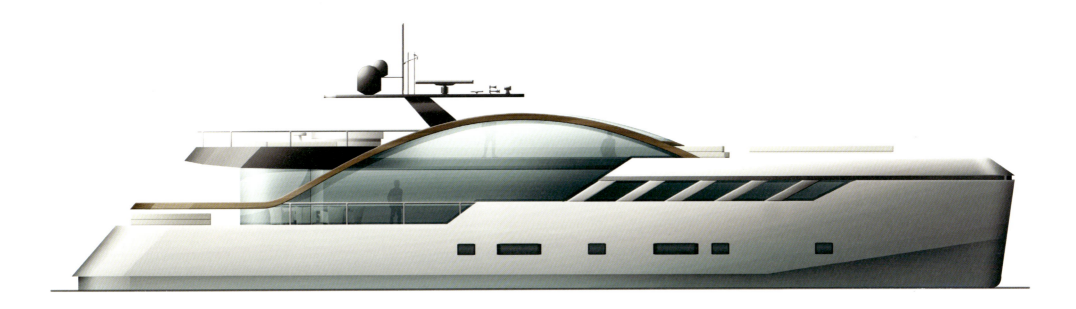
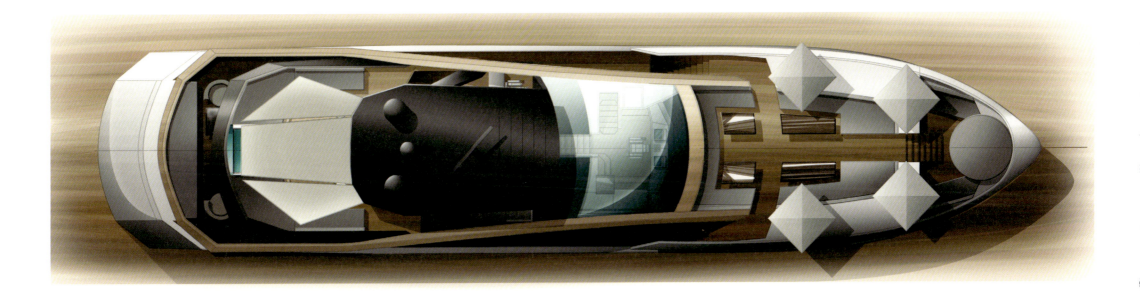

DESIGN   AIRPLANES

TOLUCA INTERNATIONAL AIRPORT HANGAR

TOLUCA, STATE OF MEXICO, MEXICO

WATCHES

I am very pleased to share with my friend Francisco López Guerra the conviction that: "No Tradition, No Future" but also: "No innovation, No Future". These beliefs have brought both of us the concept of "Fusion". Which is the connection of the past and the future, which in fact is Life and Hope!

JEAN-CLAUDE BIVER
CEO OF HUBLOT

IL ARCHITETTO HUBLOT WATCH
LIMITED EDITION

COMPETITIONS

MEXICO CITY
HOSPITAL GENERAL

MEXICO CITY, MEXICO

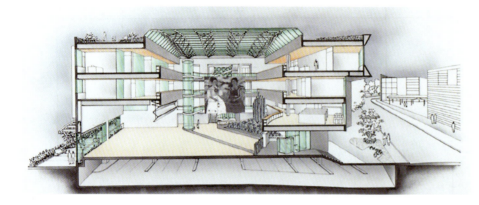
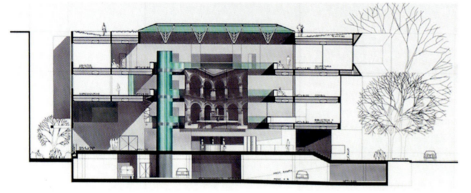
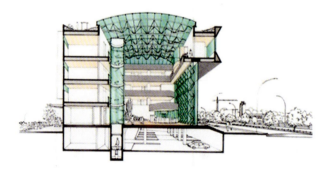

MEXICAN EMBASSY IN BERLIN PROPOSAL

BERLIN, GERMANY

HOUSE OF CONGRESS
XALAPA

XALAPA, VERACRUZ, MEXICO

MARTIN LUTHER KING MEMORIAL
WASHINGTON, DC, USA

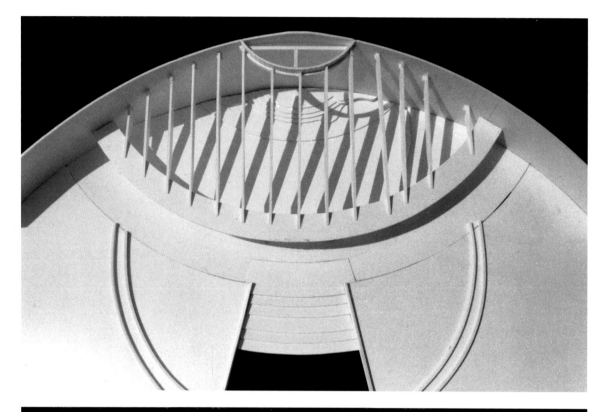

THE PARISH CHURCH OF OUR LADY OF GUADALUPE

RURAL MILFORD, INDIANA, USA

ARCO BICENTENARIO
MEXICO CITY, MEXICO

The competition was for a commemorative bridge-arch over Reforma Avenue. Not for a senseless stele.

CONJUNTO URBANO INMOBILIARIA DIO, S.A.

LEÓN, GUANAJUATO, MEXICO

SANTANDER CENTRAL OFFICE MEXICO

MEXICO CITY, MEXICO

NEW MEXICO CITY INTERNATIONAL AIRPORT

MEXICO CITY, MEXICO

The Federal Government called the competition for the NAICM. They choose Mexican architectural firms selected at the national level to be associated with international firms with experience building airports. I invited the firm JAHN, led at the time by F. González, who added his experience, as well as Alonso de Garay's Taller ADG. We appreciate Pablo Cortina's experience and knowledge of the subsoil. He made our foundation proposal for lightweight structures supported on a low-load-bearing terrain possible.

The public library of Guadalajara University was a significant experience for us. We worked very hard on the proposal as a literal and metaphorical door to knowledge and to the cultural complex of the Guadalajara University, where it is located. The building's function was to house the collection and to allow the circulation of a large number of users. Managing natural, skylight, filtered, and controlled light was a huge challenge, as a library is a place for enlightenment, and not a shadowy place for obscurantism. The rendering below shows the architectural section where one can observe the importance of the zenithal lighting that floods the internal space. This solution was undoubtedly what gave us the chance to win the international competition and build the project. However, at the last moment, the owner of the property decided to change the facade without our consent. So even if you are a worthy victor, there are battles that you can't win.

NEW PUBLIC LIBRARY OF JALISCO
MEXICO CITY, MEXICO

For more than fifteen years I have had the opportunity and the satisfaction of developing at least twenty public competitions with Pancho LópezGuerra, of which we have won several significant ones. It has been an intense collaborative work and I have been a witness to his passion and drive for the projects to achieve the highest quality.

I have also seen how he reacts with humor and optimism to the difficult challenge of losing a contest, something not very common among architects, who tend to think they deserve all the awards and recognition.

The most powerful ingredient of his work is memory. When discussing with Pancho how to define a concept for a project, you need a lot of creativity; you need to speak with the language of ideas and dreams, a language charged first and foremost with memory.

His ability to coordinate a team and consolidate it over the years is remarkable: he always knows how to join forces with the rest, and make the most of everyone to produce the best possible outcome. This is a quality that I admire, and that I have been privileged to share, because the projects we have created are, without a doubt, the product of teamwork, a team always willing to go one step further; this is the quality that for him symbolizes the four-leaf clover—the *quadrifoglio*—which he took from another of his passions: Alfa Romeo cars.

Also, his talent for coordinating and directing the construction of many of his works makes him a very rounded professional, like the old-school architects from the past who were trained to build their designs.

The proof is in the extensive list of Loguer's work, covering many scales and typologies.

ARCHITECT ANTONIO TOCA

ANTONIO TOCA
IN MEMORIAM
1943–2021

All of a sudden, this pandemic took our dear friend away. He was our associate in multiple projects and always a wise advisor. A great connoisseur of history and international architecture, a historian of our profession like few others and author of many publications, he was always a great promoter of this book. I am very grateful he was able to write this text a few days before he was infected. Above all, we enjoyed immensely his interesting and passionate friendship and his company that made our profession gratifying.

We will always miss him.
Our studio and associates deeply regret his loss.

1943 – January 12, 2021

PRODUCTION MANAGEMENT

JORGE BORBOLLA ALTAMIRANO
Architecture and museography coordinator
We have worked together since 1989

FRANCISCO JAVIER ORNELAS FAZ
Institutional projects and relations coordinator
We have worked together since 1989

GEORGINA LÓPEZGUERRA LARREA
Education and social impact
Specific projects and contests since 1989

XAVIER PRIETO DE LA BARRA
Architectural design
We have worked together since 1989

ISABEL HINOJOSA QUIRÓS
Graphic design
We have worked together since 2010

JOSÉ PABLO BALLESTEROS MARTÍNEZ PARENTE
Architectural design, interior design, and finishing coordinator
We have worked together since 2002

ALFREDO HERNÁNDEZ NERI
Architectural design, documentation, and production
We have worked together since 1995

ROBERTO GATICA JIMÉNEZ
Architectural design and consultant coordinator
We have worked together since 2006

ANTONIO TOCA
Member of the Board

FRANCISCO LÓPEZGUERRA LARREA
Development and project coordinator
Member of the Board

CARLOS BETANZO L.
Member of the Board

LOGUER | MUSEOTEC TEAM

CONSULTANTS

Augusto Fernando Álvarez Fuentes
Pablo Eduardo Álvarez Rico
Carlos Arellano Valdez
Eduardo Briones Ramírez
Julián Brody
César Calixto Díaz
Oscar Camacho Barco
Carlos Cervantes
Eduardo Manuel Chay
Miguel Ángel Flores Merino
Efrén Franco Morales
Eduardo Garibay Guerra
Andrés Giovanini
Jacobo Gorodezky
Luis Kasuga O.
Georgina Larrea Mota Velasco
Francisco López Bayghen
Miguel López Juárez
Hugo Malo Cubera
Ariel de Jesús Méndez Brindis
Manuel Montes de Oca Ramírez
Esperanza Munguia
Mario Muñoz Molina
Eduardo Olbes Ortigas
Francisco Pérez de Salazar
Haydee Rovirosa
Mauricio Ruiz Galindo
Erick Sakal Lemaire
Jorge Silva Alegría
Kunihiro Takeda
Octaviano Tapia Torres
Antonio Toca Fernández
Francisco J. Treviño Lostanau
César Urrutia Sánchez
Adolfo Zaldivar Romero
Noé Andrés Zenteno Carbajal

TEAM

José Luis Albarrán Machuca
José Pablo Ballesteros Martínez Parente
Carlos Betanzo Liceaga
Jorge Borbolla Altamirano
Roberto Gatica Jiménez
Alfredo Hernández Neri
Isabel Hinojosa Quirós
Georgina Larrea Mota Velasco
Francisco LópezGuerra L.
Georgina LópezGuerra L.
Francisco Javier Ornelas Faz
David Pérez Macías
Xavier Prieto de la Barra
Francisco Reyes Huerta
Lázaro Reyes Huerta
Salvador Serralde Vega

COLLABORATORS

Felipe Aguilar Castro
Pablo Álvarez Rico
Jorge Ambrosi
Luz Artigas Aspe
Jorge Arzamendi
Tiburcio Balloys
Elizabeth Bandala Braun
Federico Barrón López
César Becerra
Magdalena Becerril
Martha Becerril
Miguel A. Becerril
Christian Benedi Pellicer
Miguel Berdeja
Daniel Blasquez
Antonio Bouffier
Manuel Braverman
Ramón Burillo Arroyo
José Mario Calero
José Luis Calixto Díaz
Humberto Carrillo
Joaquín Carrión
Sandra Cerezo
Isidro Cerqueda Cruz
Andrea Concha del Río
Gerardo Contreras Pérez
Gabriel Cortés

Isabel Curiel
Juan de Asco del Rincón
Daniel Aarón de la Fuente Guevara
Alfonso de la Piedra
José Ignacio del Cueto
Mariano del Cueto
Luis del Moral
Verónica Delgado
Salvador Díaz
Marina Patricia Díaz Herrera
Diego Dirinaldis
Bioney Domínguez
Bioney Domínguez López
Begoña Dosal Amezcua
Stephan Drolla
Luis Elizalde
Miguel Escalona
Javier Espinosa Castro
Carlos Espinosa de los Monteros
Gustavo Espinoza
Leonardo Fernández Borja
Ulises Flores
Carlos Flores Orozco
Carlos Flores Vargas
Jorge Flores Villasana
Rodrigo Frías Mier
Joel Vidal Gallardo Ceja
Ramiro Gamboa
Alonso García Cano

Santiago García de Letona Velasco
Andrea Garibay Pindter
Alejandro Gayou Almada
Guillermo Gerzabek
Ricardo Gómez
Ricardo Gómez García
Octavio González Volbre
Francisco Haggembeck
Marcos Hernández
Diana Hernández Cordero
Luis Gerardo Herrera
Alejandra Humara Gálvez
Gerardo Ibarrola
Sofía Guadalupe Iturbide Siles
Rita Izunza Mohedano
Rudy Lara
Beatriz Larrea Zepeda Carranza
Santiago Legorreta
Santiago Legorreta Cortina
Edgar León Tovar
Agustín Malanco
Violeta Mariscal
Verónica Martínez
Adriana Martínez de Alva
Alan Daniel Martínez García
Valentín Martínez Martínez
Daniel Martínez Sosa
Gerardo Maya
Helena Melgar

Lourdes Mercado
Alonso Miranda
Martín Montes de Oca
Yvonne Morales Traulsen
Leopoldo Moreno
Leopoldo Nava
Genaro Nieto
Juan Carlos Nieto
Alejandra Noble
Gisela Noble
Teresa Noble
Ramón Ocejo Alonso
Arturo Ochoa
Fernando Ojeda Ruiz
Rocío Olivares
Fátima Orendain Almada
Francisco Ortiz
Fernando Padilla
Juliana Padilla
Víctor Palacio
José Manuel Paredes
Rebeca Pereira
Ernesto Pérez
Griselda Pérez
Gabriela Pérez Ríos
Leobardo Pérez Romero
Gonzalo Pindter Ayala
Oscar Pinto
Alejandro Ramírez

José Manuel Ramírez
Mayolo Ramírez
Angélica Ramos Saavedra
Álvaro Rayón Miranda
Liliana Reyes
Víctor Reyes
Felipe Reyes Huerta
Octavio Rivera
Pablo Rivero
Manuel Rodríguez
Sandra Rodríguez Martínez
Adrián Patricio Rojo de la Vega Muñoz de Cote
Jaquelin Rojo Pérez
Antonio Romero González Castro
José Fernando Romero Luna
Ana María Ruiz
Arturo Ruiz Dueñas
Neda Saad Alcaraz
Mauricio Salazar
Raul Salazar
Armando Salazar Valdez
Carlos Alfonso Salgado
Leticia Salinas
Alejandro Sánchez
Alfredo Sánchez
José Antonio Sánchez
Marco Antonio Sánchez
María Luisa Sánchez
José Antonio Sánchez Muñiz

Berenice Sanders Boneta
Rodrigo Segovia
Verónica Servin
Giorgio Simone
Ricardo Solar
Hilda Solórzano Pérez
Begoña Sordo Ramos
Francisco Soto
Sebastián Soto
Enrique Rolando Soto Cabrera
Sergio Soto Estrada
Sergio Soto González
Alfonso Soto Soria
Diego Tamez Lappe
Alejandra Terán Morales
Ricardo Thompson
Juan Pablo Trujillo
Juan Francisco Uribe Preciado
Milagros Vargas
Ricardo Vargas
Alejandro Vázquez
Rodrigo Vélez Alcocer
Edgar Venegas Chávez
Luis Villafranca
Rocío Villanueva
Betzabet Vivanco
Carlos Viveros
Esteban Egbertus Waller Vigil
Berenise Weber

A pessimist sees the difficulty in every opportunity; an optimist sees the opportunity in every difficulty.

WINSTON CHURCHILL

With this book, I wanted to recall this last part of my life, this last section of about twenty years of work. While crossing a difficult road to recover my health, I would not have been able to make it through without the love and company of Gina, the affection of my children Francisco, Georgina, and Javier, Fernando and Ale, the joy of my grandchildren, and the good wishes and prayers of so many friends who bothered to send me their good wishes and loving gifts.

I would not have been able to make it through without the living example of my parents who I miss so much, and the cherished memories of the time I was fortunate to share with them. From those times I remember my mother's joy for life and my father's courage and strength. I remember them talking about their travels, many of them to Italy, and the friends they made there, especially Commendatore Orlando Crotti, who treated me with filial affection.

This photo summarizes my passion for design that in Italy I always found linked to my profession as an architect. Design is involved in everything they do, mainly in the automotive industry: its history and technological advances always go hand in hand with designing spaces as a line that evidences aerodynamic effects.

I have rebuilt Alfas that belonged to my father, the same ones that for years I wanted to take to the Mille Miglia, where they did not allow them according to regulations. But I was stubborn, and I made it. I had the good fortune to meet Vico Camozzi—now a great friend—who lent me his Lancia B24 to be able to compete. Then, thanks to ambassador Juan José Guerra's intervention, as well as to the active role of the Pirelli factory, especially its director, Khaled Jnifen, and the priceless support of Commendatore Orlando Crotti's family, we (Tinaco Artigas, his family, Gina, and I) had the time of our lives on that tour.

You can't describe passion, you can only live it.
ENZO FERRARI

TODO EMPIEZA Y TODO ACABA
   ES LA VIDA

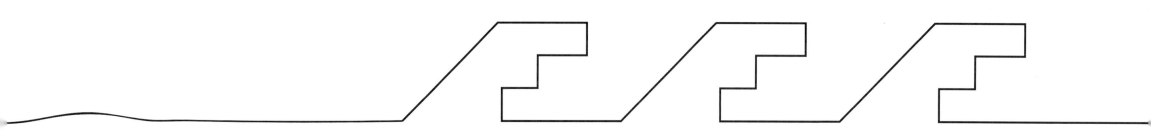

MAMY GENARO ALE FER NACHO

LA NOSTALGIA E IL AMORE QUE RIMANE

Failure is inevitable at some point in life, but giving up is unforgivable.

JB

2021-1967
=
54 YEARS

The power of architecture resides in the emotion that arises when walls, ceiling, and floor embrace light, an invisible sculpture.

FRANCISCO LÓPEZGUERRA ALMADA